THE STUDENTS OF DEEP SPRINGS COLLEGE

THE STUDENTS OF DEEP SPRINGS COLLEGE

Photographs by

Michael A. Smith

Essay by

L. Jackson Newell

Afterword by

William T. Vollmann

LODIMA PRESS
REVERE, PENNSYLVANIA

LIBRARY OF CONGRESS CONTROL NUMBER: 00–091146

ISBN 1–888899–02–6 (Hardcover Edition)
ISBN 1–888899–03–4 (Special Edition)

PRINTED IN BELGIUM

#45767951

To the students of Deep Springs College

TABLE OF CONTENTS

PREFACE

IN AUGUST OF 1993, my wife, the photographer Paula Chamlee, and I were photographing in the Ancient Bristlecone Pine Forest in the White Mountains of eastern California,
the home of the world's oldest trees. We had driven there, as we had several times before,
from the Owens Valley to the west. In the past, we had left the Ancient Bristlecone Pine
Forest by driving back the way we had come, but on this trip the Bristlecones were our last
stop for photographing, and we were heading eastward and back home to Pennsylvania. We
had been on the road since March.

While Paula was stowing her equipment, I studied the map and noticed that east of
Westgard Pass near the California–Nevada border there was a dot marked "Deep Springs
College." I called to Paula, "Hey, come look at this. There's a college on the other side of
the pass, out in the middle of nowhere, at least 30 or 40 miles from the nearest town. What
kind of college do you think it could be?" Paula guessed that, if indeed there was a college
out there, it must be either a small college involved with experimental agriculture, or one
connected to a university. We were having a hard time believing that there could be a college of any sort so remotely located, and after a brief discussion we decided that the map
was probably in error.

An hour later, as we descended from Westgard Pass, we could see a speck of green oasis
way off in the distance in the midst of the gold and brown tones of the high desert landscape. There was something anomalous out there. Fifteen miles later we came to a dirt road
with a small sign reading, "Deep Spgs Ranch." Although later in the day we were supposed
to rendezvous with a friend, we turned in, feeling curious to see what kind of place this
was, and also thinking, "Why not? This won't take long." Ahead of us were fields of hay and
alfalfa, which seemed to confirm our original suspicion that this might be an agricultural
college.

After about a mile, we passed through an open gate, crossed a cattle guard, passed a sign
that announced, "Deep Springs College," and saw some brochures set in a crude holder
nailed to a post. The brochures were obviously for the curious—like us. One was provided
for birders and was about the surprisingly abundant avian life; the other was a short description of the college itself. While we were reading and debating whether to investigate further,
a fellow came bicycling out of the main campus area, greeted us, and asked if we needed
help. As it turned out, Christopher Campbell, an alumnus, was the lawyer for the college and
was visiting Deep Springs for a weekend meeting.

An hour-long conversation ensued and we learned, with amazement that strained
credulity, about what is certainly the most unusual college in the United States. We learned
that this two-year, all-male school, founded in 1917, is primarily student run. Within broad
parameters established by the President and the Board of Trustees, the students hire and fire

the faculty, design the curriculum, select the incoming students, do the work on the school's certified organic farm and ranch (although they depend on professional ranch and farm managers), cook many of the meals (under the guidance of a chef from the Culinary Institute of America), work in the office, and generally maintain the school. That was surprising enough, but then we learned that the up to twenty-six students (it is a *very* small school) are invited to apply from among the top two percent of College Board score achievers. We then learned that, after their two years at Deep Springs, the students usually finish their undergraduate educations at universities such as Harvard, Cornell, and the University of Chicago.

Eventually, when we ran out of questions for Chris, he asked what we did. When we told him that we were artist-photographers, he suggested that we apply to teach at Deep Springs. He said they often hired faculty in the arts for a one-term (seven-week) period. Paula thought that I might want to apply. I had taught photography from 1967 through 1974 but had stopped so that I could devote myself full-time to making my own photographs. Being an unreconstructed romantic, I had wanted to make my living solely from the sale of my art. Musing out loud, I mentioned to Chris that if I were to teach a seven-week photography course at Deep Springs, I wouldn't want to limit it to a "how-to" course but would want to include things such as discussions about the nature of photographic vision and how it differs from normal seeing. Chris replied that the students might ask questions on the order of, "How does photographic vision relate to what Aristotle said about the nature of perception and reality?"

Right then I knew that if I taught a course at Deep Springs College, I could be in over my head—it had been over thirty years since I had read Aristotle, and I had forgotten most of what I'd read. Nonetheless, being challenged in this way interested me, for here I could not only teach what I loved but probably also learn something. The following winter I sent a proposal to the student-run curriculum committee to teach a seven-week course in September and October of 1995—over a year-and-a-half in the future. Not only would this be an exciting opportunity to teach brilliant and serious students, but it would also provide Paula and me with an opportunity to spend time in eastern California where we could revisit Death Valley, Owens Valley, the east side of the Sierra, and the Ancient Bristlecone Pine Forest.

My proposal was accepted, and Paula and I arrived at Deep Springs in mid-September 1995. At first, on the days when I wasn't teaching, we took photographing trips into the mountains, ranging as far as two hundred miles into the high country in Yosemite. After that first week, however, we became so caught up in the life of the college that we abandoned our photographic adventure trips for the adventure of daily life on the ranch. Each day we became increasingly interested in the highly charged mix of diverse personalities, nationalities, and ages—all isolated in a desert outpost and committed to creating a vital and humanitarian community. Through my involvement with my class and, indeed, with all the students, I realized that to be absent for even part of my limited time at Deep Springs would be to miss a valuable and irretrievable experience.

When I first came to Deep Springs, I thought I would be photographing the magnificent nearby landscape. But because of my ever-increasing involvement in the daily life at Deep Springs, I decided to attempt to make a photographic portrait of the college. Because at Deep Springs the students *are* the college to a degree unapproached by any other college or university, I determined that my portrait of Deep Springs would take the form of portraits of its twenty-five students, and that I would make two portraits of each student—a more or less formal one and and an environmental one.

I asked each student to write "something autobiographical" to accompany the more formal portrait. In the environmental portrait each student is shown in the context of some activity related to his life at the school. Many of these photographs concern an aspect of the work assignment each of them had at the time, and some relate to the student's favorite place or activity. To accompany this portrait, I asked each student to write "something brief about his experience at, or relationship to, the school."

The President of Deep Springs College, Dr. L. Jackson Newell, probably knows more about the college than anyone else. He has been involved with Deep Springs in many ways— as a student, as a faculty member, as a member of the Board of Trustees, and now as President. For this book he offered to write about the history and philosophy of Deep Springs. His introduction completes this first portrait of this most unusual and exemplary institution.

In the afterword, noted author and former Deep Springs student, William T. Vollmann writes about some of his experiences at the college and how they have shaped his life, thereby demonstrating that an education at Deep Springs goes far beyond the academic.

This book is the result of the efforts of many people to whom I am extremely grateful. First, I would like to thank Jack Newell, who has been wonderfully enthusiastic and cooperative from the beginning and whose fine essay adds a dimension that the photographs alone could not achieve. My thanks also to William T. Vollmann, who, with little notice, took time from his travels and writing to contribute his memoir. The students of Deep Springs made themselves available to be photographed in the midst of their busy schedules and sent their writing to me in a timely way. Without their full cooperation, this book would have remained only an idea. I cannot thank them enough. I would also like to thank Richard Trenner for his sensitive editing of the text. His thoughtful and often brilliant insights helped make this a much finer book than it would otherwise have been. Last, I wish to thank my wife, Paula Chamlee, who is my best critic. Her sage counsel at every stage in the making of this book has been invaluable.

MICHAEL A. SMITH
Ottsville, Pennsylvania
February 2000

DEEP SPRINGS

Education of the Students, by the Students, and for the Students

The Place and the Idea

TWENTY-EIGHT MILES EAST OF BIG PINE, CALIFORNIA, I turned off State Route 168 onto the narrow desert road marked "Deep Springs Ranch 1 Mile." Moments later my car rumbled across the cattle guard into the cottonwood-shaded oasis of the cattle ranch. A circle of attractive, wide-eaved buildings was nestled amidst expansive alfalfa fields. This is Deep Springs College. And that was four years ago. It was also over forty years ago. In 1956, I came as a new student; in 1995, I came as the new president. Why did I return to this remote and beautiful high desert valley tucked between the great wall of the Sierra and the Nevada state line? I came back because this radical experiment in liberal education had not only shaped my life but had also inspired and energized my three-decade career as a university professor.

Paradoxes abound at Deep Springs. It is at once a bold twentieth century experiment in higher education and a throwback to the ancient origins of universities. Medieval Italian universities, such as Bologna and Padua, began nearly 800 years ago when students formed guilds or self-governing unions and hired master scholars to teach them. So serious were many of these young scholars that some required their favorite tutors to seek their permission to marry (for fear marital bliss might interfere with their teaching) or to post bond before leaving town (to ensure that they returned to the university). Deep Springs is, in a sense, a re-creation of these radical beginnings (minus the meddling in professors' personal affairs). The college works, sometimes brilliantly, because students, once again, are at the center of things.

I returned to Deep Springs in the midst of a rewarding professorial career because I believe in what happens here. I now share responsibility for the integrity of the college with twenty-six undergraduate men who take their complex responsibilities with the utmost seriousness. Many of them perform their duties with near-professional expertise. After two years at Deep Springs, they transfer as juniors to complete their undergraduate degrees at such universities as Chicago, Cornell, Harvard, Michigan, Stanford, and Yale. Nearly sixty percent of the alumni have earned doctoral degrees. The majority of them pursue careers in education, health, diplomacy, and other service professions, and many render voluntary service within their communities. Little wonder that most Deep Springers (as students and alumni are called) cross that cattle guard and resume their lives "beyond the valley" with uncommon confidence that they can succeed. More significantly, they believe they can make a difference in a world that yearns for authenticity, community, and hope.

Deep Springs takes sound principles of teaching and learning to their practical limits. No tuition or fees are levied, but strenuous effort and selfless service are expected. Learning is pursued as a critical tool for the solution of real problems as well as for the sheer joy of exploration and understanding. This is, after all, a college where students take the lead in choosing the faculty who teach them, designing the curriculum, running the student admissions process, deciding whether their peers should be invited to return for a second year, and writing and editing official publications. The students also cook dinner for the entire school community, manage the library and bookstore, and govern the conduct of their own members. Equally central to the educational philosophy and practices of Deep Springs, the students carry out and typically become highly skilled at most of the labor needed to operate a certified organic farm and cattle ranch. Under the direction of an elected student labor commissioner (or foreman), they milk the cows, herd the cattle, irrigate the fields, mow the hay, and operate the heavy equipment.

Deep Springs' long history demonstrates that when students are given responsibility— serious responsibility—they rise to the challenge. The students are able, and their numbers are small. But as the college experience elsewhere becomes less personal and student motivation gives way all too often to apathy and alienation, there is at least one school that demonstrates both the feasibility and viability of a participatory alternative to top-down higher education.

Who are today's Deep Springers, and how are they chosen? As a two-year, full-scholarship, liberal arts college for men, Deep Springs receives about 200 complete applications each year. The number is relatively small for three reasons: Selection criteria are known to be stiff; college life at Deep Springs is ascetic by any standard; applicants must write seven serious essays in addition to following typical admission procedures in order to merit full consideration. The student Applications Committee invites approximately forty finalists to spend three days at Deep Springs (in groups of three); during this time each finalist is expected to participate fully in the academic and labor programs, as well as face his potential peers in an hour-long interview. When the finalists have completed their visits, the Applications Committee recommends about thirteen for admission. About ninety-five percent of those offered admission accept it. While no standardized test scores or grade point average cut-off levels are used in screening applicants, academic achievement is lofty among those admitted. The average SAT score among members of incoming classes is about 1500.

Highly qualified academically, new students join their second-year peers in the remote desert valley on July 1 each year—ready to embrace an educational program far broader than academics alone. By virtue of the admission process, the incoming Deep Springers have already demonstrated the capacity to excel in the classroom. They are now asked to accept serious practical and ethical challenges as well.

Not long before he died in 1925, the founder of Deep Springs, L. L. Nunn, expressed his charge to the student body in unequivocal language:

Gentlemen, For what came ye to the desert? Not for conventional scholastic training; not for ranch life; not to become proficient in commercial or professional pursuits for personal gain. You came to prepare for a life of service, with the understanding that superior ability and generous purpose would be expected of you, and this expectation must be justified. Even in scholastic work, average results obtained in ordinary school will not be satisfactory. The desert speaks. Those who listen will hear the purpose, philosophy, and ethics of Deep Springs, for it will need no prodding from teachers . . . to produce superior results in all departments.

L. L. Nunn and the Emergence of the Idea

Few who know about Deep Springs fail to develop a compelling curiosity about Nunn and the origin of his educational ideas. Recently I made a pilgrimage to Telluride, Colorado, where he developed his banking, mining, and hydroelectric enterprises in the 1880s and 1890s. He made the bulk of his fortune as an inventor and entrepreneur in hydroelectric power generation and, more importantly, in long-distance power transmission.

In 1891, with the support of the Western Electric Company, Nunn was the first to demonstrate that alternating current (AC) could be transmitted by wires over a distance of many miles. In this pioneering effort, Nunn built a power plant at Ames on the San Miguel River in southwestern Colorado and sent the current over high tension lines to his stamp mills at the Gold King Mine in the Silver Mountains. This breakthrough soon revolutionized industrial production by separating the use of electrical power from the power source.

At the entrance to the Elks Park in the center of Telluride, L. L. Nunn's striking image still greets you today. There, a monument commemorates his achievements in mining, hydroelectric power, and alternating current transmission. In the mountains around Telluride the ghosts of the Alta, Ophir, and Gold King mines linger on. The rebuilt Ames and Bridal Veil power stations remain as living monuments, and Nunn's well-kept home still stands on the corner of Columbia and Aspen Streets. Next to it stands the Cornell House. He built this modest but attractive two-story dwelling to house some of the young technicians who were in training to run his power plants. Appropriately, the Cornell House was the first home ever constructed with built-in wiring for electric lights. The old ceramic post-and-tube wiring is visible through recently installed glass panels in the ceiling.

The old San Miguel Bank, which Butch Cassidy and his gang rifled for $35,000 in their first bank robbery, still stands across the street from the Nunn monument. The bank president at the time happened to be L. L. Nunn, who owned a swift horse and knew how to ride it. He quickly organized a posse and led the chase. The diminutive Nunn left the posse in his dust and quickly overtook Cassidy on a mountain trail. The bandit promptly turned on Nunn and unhorsed him, stole his faster horse, and left him to be found by his men. Clearly, Nunn was not your typical banker or entrepreneur. From this multifaceted Telluride beginning as a banker, miner, and hydroelectric developer, his enterprises spread throughout the West and eventually also included the installation of the Niagara Falls power plant—which continues in operation nearly a century after Nunn built it. My few days in historic Telluride put Nunn's entrepreneurial and educational legacy in a new light.

Innovation and responsibility were at the core of Nunn's philosophy, and he felt they should be at the center of a good society. As tuberculosis began to sap his strength, and as age started to take its toll, he worried about where future leaders of vision and courage would come from. After establishing his power plants throughout Utah, Colorado, and beyond, he began to experiment more broadly with worker education. At his Olmsted Power Station in Provo Canyon, Utah, he hired bright young men and trained them on the job to operate the generators and to manage the plant. He was now becoming interested in the moral development and social consciousness of his protegés. He soon supplemented the practical instruction he offered with study in the liberal arts. Nunn built a stately, three-story educational facility next to the Olmsted Power Station and offered free room, board, and study space to professors on sabbatical from nearby colleges. In exchange, he solicited their agreement to tutor his "pinheads" in history, literature, and philosophy. "Pinheads" became a popular nickname for Nunn's young workers, not because they were bright and often studious, but because, as he moved them around during their apprenticeships, he kept track of them with labeled pins on a large map of the Great Basin.

One step remained in Nunn's educational odyssey. If on-the-job study of electrical engineering was turning his young power plant workers into resourceful managers, then humanities concepts such as justice, mercy, and human dignity might also come alive if students could put them into practice in real situations. As part of a complex effort, he granted a large measure of autonomy to the "pinheads" at each of his Telluride Power Company schools—and expected them, in return, to work, study, and govern their own affairs in a cooperative manner. The more tangible and complete the responsibility given them, Nunn reasoned, the more they would learn about leadership and the better they would understand the needs of others and the demands of citizenship. Generating electricity became a secondary interest; Nunn was now consumed with pursuing his new educational mission. Telluride Power generated the funds with which to underwrite these educational experiments.

By 1911, Nunn's business partners were weary of what they regarded as his expensive "educational diversions." Telluride stockholders wanted an annual report with big dividends, not a literary journal produced by its workers at the power plant in Beaver, Utah. Irritated by the unappreciative response to what he saw as his moral vision and daring spirit, Nunn sold his interest in the Telluride Power Company and used the proceeds to found the Telluride Association. *This* Telluride was all about education. Through the Association, Nunn built a large house on the Cornell University campus in Ithaca, New York. This building became known as the Telluride House at Cornell. Offering room and board scholarships to former pinheads as well as to able new male recruits, Nunn created by-laws by which the student members of the Association would not only be self-governing but also act as trustees or custodians of the endowment. But Telluride House was to be the secondary branch of Nunn's educational enterprise—the place where his Cornell scholars would live and learn following two years at his yet-to-be-created primary branch for freshmen and sophomores. This primary branch was to be independent of the Telluride Association and of Cornell University and offer an educational experience that combined theory and practice in every facet. Agriculture, not business, would provide its practical foundation.

In 1916, Nunn established a tiny two-year men's college or "primary branch" on a farm near Claremont, Virginia, just across the James River estuary from Williamsburg. It failed the test of remoteness due to the allure of social attractions in town, and he closed the school in less than a year. Lamenting this failure to an old friend, the Chicago business executive Albert M. Johnson, he mentioned the need for a remote location if he were to make a second attempt. Johnson had an idea. He was the invisible partner behind Death Valley Scotty, the witty prospector with whom he built the famous desert castle near the California – Nevada border. Frequently vacationing *incognito* at the castle, Johnson knew the area well and suggested that Nunn consider buying the lonely Stewart Ranch in Deep Springs Valley, which was for sale.

The two men took an automobile trip there in the spring of 1917. Nunn was struck by the beauty and solitude of the site and purchased the property immediately. Stonemasons were soon at work on prairie-style college buildings inspired by the work of architect Frank Lloyd Wright. The first class of students arrived—many from the East Coast—that October. Their first task, while they camped in tents, was to finish construction of the Main Building, library, faculty bungalows, and boarding house.

Three Pillars: Putting an Idea into Practice

Education at Deep Springs is based on three well-balanced elements: academic study, agricultural and community labor, and service through democratic decision-making. Daily life integrates all three elements to prepare students for a life of service. The communal existence, coupled with the desert isolation, also lays claim to everyone's time and energy from dawn to late evening, seven days a week. It is a strenuous life—physically, intellectually, and emotionally taxing.

The Deep Springs day begins before 6:00 A.M. Those responsible for milking the dairy cows and feeding the farm animals begin work before sunrise. So do members of the dining room crew, and, of course, those who rise early to study or to perform other essential farm and ranch tasks. In addition, moving irrigation lines in the alfalfa fields, mowing and baling hay, or assisting with the birth of a calf can summon community members to their labors at any time of day or night.

A large bell mounted outside the boarding house calls the community to breakfast at 7:30. The food is hearty, often prepared with home-grown beef, although vegetarian dishes are always available. Conversations over meals range from world events—as reported in the two-days-late *New York Times*—to Deep Springs' own problems or controversies. All this is peppered with the wry humor of people who share so much time together.

The morning hours are devoted chiefly to academic work. Students attend classes, write papers, and do their homework. Four to six students constitute the typical class, and the Socratic method of questioning and conversing about possible answers defines the pedagogy. The unprepared student is embarrassed; the unprepared instructor is mortified. Faculty members tend to be near the beginning or end of their careers, since Deep Springs cannot offer academic tenure. Three long-term professors serve for up to six years, and three short-term faculty lines are occupied by different visiting professors every semester. As president, I teach regularly, too, and the other staff members often teach classes in their specialties—from horsemanship to large-engine repair, from gourmet cooking to sustainable agriculture. The student-led Curriculum Committee writes and revises the academic program and recommends faculty hiring. Maintaining full accreditation is not the only incentive: students know their chances of transferring to the university of their choice depend on their safeguarding the educational integrity and reputation of Deep Springs.

At 12:30, the bell rings again and lunch is served. The conversation in the dining room is abuzz with ideas from the classroom and focused on problems to be solved on afternoon labor projects. The student Labor Commissioner announces any last-minute adjustments in work assignments needed to meet emergency situations—a failing windmill on a hot summer day, an accounting error in the student-run bookstore that might delay the arrival of texts for next term's courses, or fifty cows in danger of bloating from green alfalfa because a gate was not latched properly. Students fan out to perform their labor assignments or to tackle any special problems. The Labor Commissioner roams about the ranch and campus, supervising his peers, offering advice, and securing necessary materials.

At dinner, which begins at 6:00, conversations may reflect the day's challenges. Why didn't the windmill repair work? How can the bookstore's credit be protected from further mistakes? What was the value of the two cows that died in the alfalfa field, and should the person who left the gate ajar bear that cost? Just as likely, however, talk will range from whether Deep Springs should admit women, always a spirited issue, to the question to be addressed at 8:00 by the distinguished scholar in residence that week: "Who is really responsible for the atrocities in Algeria and how might they be stopped?" But before and after that lecture, the spacious Main Room may be filled with music as students prepare for a recital on Saturday night or with the Applications Committee as it meets to select the forty finalist candidates to be invited for on-campus interviews. The committee meeting may run on into the wee hours of the night. This is a typical day at Deep Springs.

But if the dinner bell rings and it isn't mealtime, an emergency exists and everyone responds. Living fifty miles from a hospital, in an area with poor mountain roads and always-vulnerable phone lines, is enough to rally even the college community's least compatible members to heroic cooperative efforts. When a senior professor suffers severe chest pains, bitter differences that erupted in a committee meeting earlier that day pale before the common desire to help him and respond to the emergency.

It is no mystery why Nunn regarded his students as the "beneficial owners" of the college. One reason tuition and fees have never been levied, despite some very lean years for the endowment, is to make it clear that students here are neither paying customers nor honored guests—unlike tuition-paying or scholarship-receiving students at other educational institutions. To make his point exceptionally clear, in the Deed of Trust, Nunn granted the student body one fully-empowered seat on the nine-member Board of Trustees. When the board expanded itself to thirteen members recently, students were granted a second seat, thereby enhancing rather than diluting their influence.

Nunn gave students both power and responsibility. In the Deed of Trust he charged them with observing two ground rules, known collectively and informally as the isolation policy. There are to be no mind-altering drugs, and no unnecessary trips to Big Pine or Bishop, California, the nearest towns. Wisely, Nunn put the student body itself in charge of defining and enforcing these ground rules. Honor and responsibility, individually and collectively, are infused throughout the educational program.

Important as rigorous scholarship, responsible labor, and participatory decision-making are to students at Deep Springs, they remain only means to an end. Responsibility for oneself, for the community, and for the land on which we depend is the essential core of the experience. The ranch and farm, for example, are essential to Deep Springs' educational program for many reasons. They offer students the chance to learn irrigation, animal husbandry, or cowboy skills. They place heavy responsibilities on students to deal with economic and practical realities. They also offer Deep Springers a rare opportunity in our society to understand the sources of life—the production of food and fiber. More importantly, however, the farm and ranch are vital because they are working laboratories, bridging theory and practice in land stewardship and sustainable agriculture.

The educational benefits of our isolated valley and surrounding mountains have been magnified with the recent development and growing effectiveness of an experimental range management team. Chaired by the Deep Springs Ranch Manager, the range management team consists of representatives from the U.S. Forest Service, Bureau of Land Management, and Soil Conservation Service; the California Department of Fish and Game; the Native Plant Society; and Deep Springs' president and several students. This cooperative approach to land stewardship has enriched our educational program while earning recognition as a promising model for range management in other environmentally sensitive areas. As we enter a century that will require reconciling the human demand for food and fiber with environmental limitations and degradation, Deep Springers may be among those who are prepared to de-polarize acrimonious stalemates and forge effective solutions to environmental, scientific, and economic problems.

The Value of the Idea in Practice

The challenges of Deep Springs do not end when a student leaves the valley. The ethic of the college remains with him. When a student accepts his full-ride scholarship, he is expected to share fully in the responsibility to create the most comprehensive liberal arts education available anywhere. He is also expected to set aside selfish interests and commit himself unstintingly to the welfare of the community. While they are in residence, Deep Springs invites its students, as well as its faculty and staff, to live by altruistic standards. When students leave the college, they are expected to dispatch their debt to the college and reflect the essence of their extraordinary learning experiences by dedicating themselves to the service of others.

The genius of the founder's approach is that he did not define service or community. Nunn, who died in 1925, put that onus on each student, faculty, and staff member. Each must hammer out his or her own definition of these ideas. Deep Springs' students, therefore, live and study with a consciousness that much has been given to them (their scholarships being only a result of their natural gifts and interests), and so a great sense of responsibility is expected of them. The quest to discover one's gifts and to apply them creatively in the real world inspires serious introspection and vigorous conversation at the college.

Deep Springs is democratic in its daily life but meritocratic in its recruitment and selection. From the beginning, admission has been based on academic excellence, personal achievement, and leadership potential, broadly defined. The college now recruits worldwide. In the last few years, the student body has included members who were reared in France, India, Japan, Korea, Lebanon, Poland, and Russia. The states with the most students in attendance now are Pennsylvania, New Jersey, Washington, and California, although the geographic origins of the students shift from one year to the next. Religious, political, and cultural diversity is especially central to this educational environment, and these contrasts within the student body are always strong. Sharp differences of opinion or judgment abound, but they are frequently buffered by spontaneous humor.

Adding to the vitality of education at Deep Springs is the authenticity of the students' labor and self-governance responsibilities. As "beneficial owners," students consider the college their own within the limits of such practical realities as legal conditions, fund raising, and long-term policy needs. With a whole college and ranch community to run and so few students to carry out the work, every job is essential and everyone knows and feels this reality. Failure to do a job, or to do it well, has a detrimental effect on everyone. If the cows are not milked on time, there is no milk on the dinner table. If a faculty candidate is not written in a timely and professional manner, she or he may be lost to the college. Personal responsibility and the natural consequences of failing to carry one's share of the load stimulate growth and maturation.

Whither Nunn's Educational Legacy?

As a professor of the history and philosophy of higher education, I have recently concentrated my research on the life cycles of progressive colleges and universities' reforms. Why do some fine experiments like Black Mountain College in North Carolina (1933-56) simply burn out? Why do others like the University of California, Santa Cruz (founded 1965) surrender their distinctive characteristics and join mainstream higher education? Why do a few like Antioch and Berea (founded in 1852 and 1855, respectively) continue after a century-and-a-half to renew their commitments and resources and pursue an independent course? Where on this spectrum—from early flame-out, through lost vision and consequent drift, to courageous self-renewal—will scholars eventually place Deep Springs?

Deep Springs is experiencing a rebirth. While the college has always been strong in its educational program, decades of deficit spending imperiled its educational quality and by 1994 placed the physical plant and endowment in mortal danger. In the last several years, with remarkable cooperation from all quarters, the college has stopped its financial hemorrhage, brought the budget into balance, and received generous assistance in rebuilding the endowment. The dilapidated and dangerous dormitory wing of the Main Building has just been replaced by a new student residence; the old Main Building itself, which Nunn built in 1917, was recently remodeled and seismically reinforced; and throughout the community the antiquated utility infrastructure is being replaced.

Conclusions

Rewarding and exciting as the fiscal and physical renewal of Deep Springs is, taken alone it amounts metaphorically to little more than the restoration of the Cornell House in Telluride, Colorado. The house may be interesting to look at, but is anything worthwhile going on there? Fundamentally, Deep Springs is an idea, not a campus, nor a college, nor a ranch. Its purpose is to prepare genuinely free individuals who commit their lives to the common good. Deep Springs practices democracy in learning, accepting risks and enduring inefficiencies that no other college would tolerate, precisely to offer its students the possibility of extraordinary growth in character and intellect. The Deep Springs community strives to keep this daring vision clear and its pursuit undiluted.

On my way back to Deep Springs following my recent sojourn in Telluride, I toured the Glen Canyon Dam in Page, Arizona, with its huge hydroelectric works. It began producing electricity for distribution across the western states in 1963. All twelve 345,000-volt generators were producing at capacity when I took the tour. From Ames, Colorado to Page, Arizona in less than three-quarters of a century: what an amazing, transforming power Nunn set in motion. Seeing the Ames and Glen Canyon hydro plants within two days of each other got me thinking. Has Deep Springs—the institution in which L.L.Nunn, looking back at the end of his life, took greatest satisfaction—merely survived like the Cornell House in Telluride? Or has it influenced higher education to anything like the same degree that his technical and entrepreneurial ideas revolutionized the power industry?

Deep Springs is a radical and continuing experiment in higher learning. Its survival, daring, and progress are important to the educational world. L.L. Nunn breathed life into a pedagogy for ethical and intellectual development that should not perish. But his ideas are endangered, still lodged in a tiny and remote niche. Meanwhile, the juggernaut of mass instruction, detached learning, and impersonal treatment defines undergraduate life in most American colleges and universities. And these conditions help breed a sense of futility and cynicism among the very people on whom a livable planetary and social climate will depend in the twenty-first century.

Those of us entrusted with responsibility for Deep Springs—the students, faculty, staff, and trustees—feel a common obligation not only to keep the idea alive (as well as the institution itself), but also to ensure that it flourishes. Deep Springs strives to demonstrate what truly responsible and democratic institutions can do to improve and enrich students' lives. It excels in preparing its students to tackle the critical educational and human problems of contemporary society.

The success of Deep Springs in setting such a standard will ensure that its students carry, naturally and effectively, the onus of L. L. Nunn's mandate to improve the moral and ethical life of the nation and world. The aim is not just to run a good college or extend its life, nor simply to demonstrate that students are capable of governing their own affairs and taking responsibility for the operation of an agricultural and academic program. Deep Springs' purpose is to inspire a few particularly able students to apply their individual and collective talents to improve a troubled society and protect an endangered planet. In a society fraught with alienation and cynicism, Deep Springs' goal is to foster an educational and community experience so vigorous, so just, and so humane that its students will hold it up as an achievable standard toward which they will strive wherever they may later serve.

L. JACKSON NEWELL
President
Deep Springs College
Deep Springs, California
January 2000

THE STUDENTS

Samuel Tregar   Cranston, Rhode Island

I was born on August 2, 1977, the eagerly awaited first child of my parents, Rosemary and Jack. We lived in Philadelphia until I was eight months old, when we moved to Rhode Island, my Dad's home state. I was raised in Cranston with my two years' younger brother, Mark, as a suburban American (Jewish) boy. We played Little League baseball and soccer; we were Cub Scouts and went to Hebrew School. I studied two forms of karate, learned to use, program, and take apart several computers, read constantly, and wrote poetry. My friends came to me for help with all sorts of instruction manuals, and we invented variations on basketball and ping-pong. Although the public school system identified me as "gifted," most of my formal education was frustrating and disappointing. Finally, I convinced my parents to enroll me in a private, alternative high school in grade 11, School One, where I found inspiration and acceptance. At 18, I have known close friendships, true love, and intellectual challenge and have learned that all three are important to me.

Samuel Tregar   Cranston, Rhode Island

Sam Tregar! Sam Tregar! The world is awaiting the appearance of a hotshot! Are you He? At one time I thought so. I came to Deep Springs a hatching hero, ready to rock the world, people and plants, dogs and houses right off the hinges. Of course, what I hadn't remembered was that there were 25 hotshots already waiting for me. We get along, and I mellow out day by day. Deep Springs is sometimes about learning to be a smaller self.

Jacob Giessman   Columbia, Missouri

I grew up in Missouri. My family hunted and killed all its meat and chopped all its firewood. We were definitely middle class but always deeply rooted in our environment. I had a mediocre education and mediocre peers, and left the Midwest in frustration.

Jacob Giessman   Columbia, Missouri

I came to Deep Springs because of a strong distaste for everyday society and an ardent desire for a community of peers I could respect. During my time here, I have outgrown my teen angst and gained a new understanding of myself. The challenge of Deep Springs has forced me out of living down to society's standards and living in perpetual dissatisfaction. I feel when I leave this valley I will have the ability to engage or reject society creatively and constructively . . . though I'm certainly in no hurry to leave Deep Springs.

I revel in the intellectual community here. I miss the forest but have grown to see the beauty of the desert. It took a year to get used to the landscape. The nude hills and desert scrub seemed at first dead and inhospitable. I grew up in a very lush environment and have had to train myself to see the tiny flowers, secretive animals, and hidden water sources of the valley. When I hike, I feel at the same time that I am naked and that no one is looking.

Nikolai Slywka   Tarrytown, New York

My family—parents and older brother—have had the same white house for twenty years and
through countless nuances of disrepair and upkeep. What can I say, I spent my time in schools, the
first five grades in the public system and the last seven in a beautiful, small, private place from which
I walked home on hot autumn days. Education was, and still is, my family's compelling dynamic. My
memories echo the rhythms of the school year, its deadlines, weekends, and prize-days. Strangely,
however, my most vivid recollection and the one that most resonates with my time at Deep Springs
occurred during a summer vacation. I had joined a friend and his father on a drive across the U.S.
While the car was being serviced at a Nevada gas station, my friend and I convinced each other to
wander toward a shabby building that our acute, twelve-year-old minds had marked as a brothel. We
entered, immediately confronted by girls in white dressing gowns, long earrings, and rouge. Perhaps
it was the heat of the day, the fear of the unknown, or the very pleasure of the sight; I turned pale
and stood still without saying a word before bolting out the door and down the road.

Nikolai Slywka   Tarrytown, New York

Seven years later I found myself in front of another Nevada brothel. I was going to Deep Springs for the first time after flying into Las Vegas the day before and spending the night in a youth hostel. Mihir and I met the next morning on the bus, easily recognizing each other as Deep Springs' students among the older, grayer passengers. After five hours of unremitting desert, the bus pulled into Lida Junction, a dusty crossroads where the Deep Springs van waited for us. A group of second year students shuffled around and told us where to put our bags. Only Frank mentioned the Cottontail Ranch that stood fifty yards away, its "open 24 hrs" sign hanging from a telephone pole. We introduced ourselves; I learned that many of the guys I'd taken for second year students were just first year students like myself who had arrived a few days earlier and acquired a somewhat deceptive self-confidence. We piled into the van, pulling away from Lida and its awful, sun-bleached expanse and toward the mountains behind which was Deep Springs.

Nathaniel Birdsall   Poughkeepsie, New York

I was born in Idaho and grew up in North Dakota, Texas, and New York. My father is a librarian with wanderlust and my mother is a violinist. I've only written five letters in the past year, and I've only gotten away from the college twice: once to San Francisco for four days, and once to go back home for a week.

Nathaniel Birdsall   Poughkeepsie, New York

Deep Springs provides a close-knit, family-like atmosphere, and, as might be expected, my relations with it are alternately rewarding and dysfunctional; when I'm in the valley I usually feel either bitter or beatific. People collide here a lot, and it's very difficult to avoid each other. It's straining to know that I've come here for a twenty-five person bumper-car ride . . . straining to know that I want to make lasting connections with the same people I periodically crave to throttle. I feel terrible when I argue and fight with someone here, but I feel even worse when I evade contact altogether.

Octavian Drulea   **Portland, Oregon**

I am an American citizen immigrated from Romania. I grew up in the sweet wooded hills of Oregon with the Pacific Ocean always nearby. In public school I was a regular kid, more or less. I received a few distinctions and honors here and there, but, more importantly, I developed a sense of humor and an imagination despite the best efforts of the institutions I attended. These I think have made it possible for me to maintain hope and courage in the face of the oncoming specter of the future and have directly resulted in my attendance here. My wish is that someday my being here will benefit more people than myself.

Octavian Drulea   Portland, Oregon

In the city, I often find merely loneliness, despite all the crowds of people. But out here in the desert there are always spirits; they make you feel at home. One doesn't have to go out very far to find them, usually just a few hundred feet out of any building here. They are of course unpredictable spirits, sometimes very frightening in fact, and I do not think that they are necessarily all together in a unified mass but probably more like a nation of individually operating spirits. Each has its own specific way of talking; some are loud, others are meek. Because of the revelations which were graciously made apparent to me by my friends the spirits of Deep Springs Valley, or the "Little Asylum of Children," as the ancient people used to call it, I have found an education I can believe in. One learns common sense out here as well as philosophy or ecology. One also learns how to teach oneself. There are a lot of strange qualities to this valley, but I suppose Deep Springs is certainly no stranger than the lands I will inhabit when I leave here, so I'm making the most of my training here before I'm plunged into the thick of the action.

Christian Von Nicholson   Helena, Montana

I was raised in a gray house on the south side of a cold and land-locked state. We siblings, four (now five), stacked into strange shapes on the broad grass, lay down at odd angles in dusky memory. I propped up my bed with dog-eared fantasy novels and fashioned myself an invisible hero between bites at the dinner table. High school, a denial of childhood and maturity, wrested little heroism from me, but the years, run together, arch over me now, like the rings of the sun, in blinding obscurity.

Christian Von Nicholson   Helena, Montana

I approached Deep Springs with a great belief in its power to shape me. At first I found I shaped it instead. I took care of the Dairy Barn, the cows, or didn't, and passed it on. Student Body meetings, grand schemes and laughter, boredom and doubt: these cushioned my ambivalence and desire. This ability, by default, to shape things gave me a sense of place.

Returning that first hot September, cresting the pass after a week's break, Deep Springs cooled my burning heart. I slowly began to perceive other hearts moving around me, and those who were once mere figures turned and sculpted me. That's why I think I'm here.

Stephen Singer   **Moorestown, New Jersey**

Born two months early without a middle name, I took an interest in dinosaurs, air compressors, grappling hooks, and Marc Chagall. I disbelieve official business and have no patience for time. On summer nights I watched the fireworks of Dad's arc welder from the Philadelphia row-house window. I have a bit of cerebral palsy, sure, but now I'm more about the phenomenology and the ethics of touch, about communication that is only lately returning to the beauty of pauses.

Stephen Singer   Moorestown, New Jersey

I came here for the people and the stars. When the student body and its dogs hiked up to the Druid,
The Valley's monolith, to welcome back our members at the end of the summer, many of us stayed
to watch the moon rise. The Valley looked like Mars. On the way up, Chris explained to me the
debate over essentialism. On the way down, Josh and I discussed our pasts, death, and love for an aging
dog. Fritz teaches me the mechanics of optimism, Seth introduces me to Bhuto and a language of
enthusiasm, John-Henry shows me the dangers of taking one's self for granted, and on, and on . . .

Joe Gardner Wessely   **Placitas, New Mexico**

I am Joe Gardner Wessely, Elizabeth Gardner's son, Jack Gardner's grandson. I am a native New Mexican, born and raised in the hills and arroyos of Las Placitas, in El Rancho de los Alamos Altos. I am half Hungarian Jew—from Budapest to New York—and I am half western American, stemming from Texas cowboys and travelers to Washington state. These Americans are all types, French Huguenot, Irish, English, Dutch, and other. Somewhere in there hides a little Comanche and a little Mexican, but polite folks in Texas didn't talk about that kind of thing, especially if it was kin. These are the externals to which I cling in hope of giving my internal some anchor, or substance.

Joe Gardner Wessely   Placitas, New Mexico

I hoped to step out of history and flee structure by coming here, looking for a place where free-dom of youth and thought could reign. I now know that it was silly to expect ahistorical sur-roundings, but now the challenge is rewriting the traditions and expectations of Deep Springs. I'd like to spend the rest of my time here discovering the disparate languages this little Babel uses and can create. I suppose I'll remember our struggles here more than anything else. Moments from the struggles for coeducation and student self-government haunt me and I wonder just what I could have done to have made them turn out better. It may be years before my sister will be allowed to attend Deep Springs and share the intense laughter and rage I shared with people like Frank and Octavian. I look forward to the day when this school no longer subscribes to a robber baron's def-inition of who can be a leader while I still look back fondly on my brief days here.

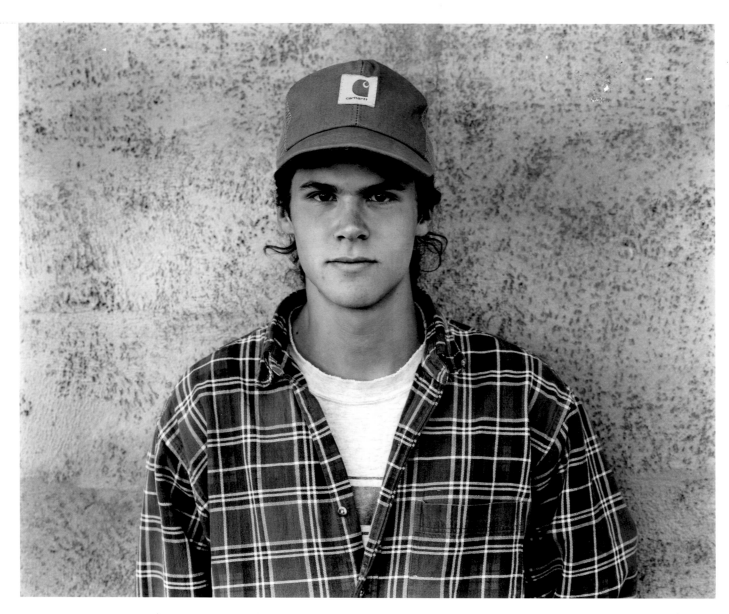

John Dewis   St. Davids, Pennsylvania

At the Haverford School, a prep school for boys in the suburbs of Philadelphia, I learned how to
decline farmer, *agricola*. At home my father helped me study this. He is a physician who works to
rehabilitate patients with head injuries. My mother and sister are physical therapists, and my other
sister is a massage therapist, as well as a sculptor and painter. At home on St. David's Road, we have
sung Christmas carols door-to-door with neighbors and have sledded down the big hill. My mom
leads the troops. She also plays the ukelele and gets us all to sing "Happy Birthday" in close har-
mony over the phone to people. Sometimes it's their birthday.

John Dewis   St. Davids, Pennsylvania

I sought Deep Springs as a community of intellectuals who were willing to meet on other-than-intellectual terms. For two years a relentless ideal has asserted itself as both the object of our study and the context in which to study it, such that the rest of the world temporarily recedes in light of occasionally mundane tasks. I sometimes worry that we will leave Deep Springs, half-arrogantly, half-guiltily, with the troubling conviction that we are privileged to understand something that no one else can. I am indebted to L.L. Nunn, the trustees, and my friends in the valley.

Lift hoof with authority and grace. Do not wrestle the beast, simply hold the leg without letting him put it back down. Rasp evenly and smoothly until even and smooth, taking more from the toe and heels than from the seat of corn. Shape the shoe on the anvil with definitive blows; if you try to shape it too perfectly you will surely bend it to hell. Hold the shoe in place on the hoof with your palm and drive a nail in a hole on each side. Bend ends over so they do not tear your hand if the horse pulls away. Hold nails in your mouth. Short taps of the hammer will make the nail curve and poke out faster and lower, long taps drive the nails up higher. Avoid quicking the horse.

Geoffrey Andersen   Anaheim, California

I was born and raised in Anaheim, California, the one-time home of endless citrus groves and the current home of Disneyland and conservative politics. Nearly all of my experiences have been formulated within the context of my home town. By the time I graduated from high school, I had only ventured beyond California's frontiers six times, mostly on excursions to Nevada or Arizona. I see this current stage of my life as a period of exploration, a being away from home. Distance has increased my esteem for my origins, but allowed me to see them more critically.

Geoffrey Andersen   Anaheim, California

Deep Springs has been a wonderful place, and I have learned a lot and enjoyed myself immensely. However, most of the knowledge I've derived from my experiences here has contributed to my life by giving me something to react against rather than respond to. In many ways, Deep Springs is what a community should never be, or maybe Deep Springs is what a community inherently is. I think the microcosmic scale of the Deep Springs community will allow me to better perceive the inter-personal interactions that are more subtly disguised in the larger world and to assume some agency in improving those relationships.

Owen Gjertsen   Raleigh, North Carolina

The token Southerner mulls over autobiography. He has heard that an artist writes his own biography, but he is having trouble. His brainstorm is a series of letters and numbers: b8/2/77145#5'10" 790M720Vh781-4114, etc. A computer reading his autobiography will appreciate it. The artist-or-not is at no lack of anecdotes of his life that read like fables of Just-So-Stories; it is all chronicled in illuminated manuscripts he has hidden away in a false tooth and you can read his spirit like tree rings with the right tools. He shows you none of this, however, sprinkling a thin film of words like dust and turning to fly away. He has left you the question about the brothers who always or never lie, but no answer. This and his two eyes are his autobiography.

Owen Gjertsen   Raleigh, North Carolina

"The sandbox analogy is good," Stephen tells me, but I can't help but think it's too negative. "It's where the kids all learn to play fair, to not make each other eat sand." *The best sandbox in America*, I think. Maybe. We are all kids here, and all boys at that, though this does not keep us from being some really great kids, and we've been working at dismantling the faded "no gurlz" sign, but the screwdrivers are all lost somewhere under the sand. By the plastic bucket, some of us are playing cowboy games, while others—*Perhaps this is the wrong analogy*, I think, and try for a while to think of a better one. A tightly knit flock of geese alone in the vast blue sky? A brilliant, sputtering torch? Deep Springs College: the best cup of black coffee you'll ever drink (?).

Franklin Zaromb   Hinsdale, Illinois

Since four students and a professor last year said they were from New Jersey, I said I was from Chicago, even though I was born in Livingston and raised my first five years in Newark. And usually instead of saying I'm from Chicago, I say I'm from Aurora, Illinois, because, as most everyone in the Western Hemisphere knows, Aurora's home to a certain special entertaining pair known as Wayne and Garth. When I introduce myself to strangers as being from Aurora, a town which I lived in for only four years, I get the chance to open the floor of our conversation to more than just an exchange of weather and sports tidbits. After a round of Wayne and Garth jokes, though, I tell them that Aurora is nothing like the movie "Wayne's World"; that I've also lived in Hinsdale, Baltimore, Livingston, and Newark; that I'm only a first generation American citizen to begin with; and that I'm a Jew before I'm any sort of geographically-bound subject.

Franklin Zaromb   Hinsdale, Illinois

High school ended sourly as I witnessed many students my age exchanging fresh disruptive curiosi-
ties for comforting guarantees of social mobility, which led me to believe that letters of college
acceptance were nothing more than financial pacts the old were forming with the young to per-
petuate the old. When I was visiting colleges, Deep Springs was an oasis of earnest intellectualism,
primarily because its students were the most idealistic students I had ever encountered (the atheists
in particular!). For them, Deep Springs appeared to be time on hold. With few academic require-
ments, financial constraints, and reminders of future graduate, medical, or law schools for students
to concern themselves with, intellectual and practical work was done more to fulfill immediate
communal obligations than to satisfy long-term individual ambitions. I saw then, as I see now, students willing to take responsibility for their actions and the idealized welfare of the community. I
chose to attend Deep Springs because Deep Springers identify themselves not as mere undergraduate students or propagators of old wealth, but as thoughtful participants in a perpetually renewed
utopian educational experiment.

Joshua Kim   Fullerton, California

Religion: Christian. Ethnicity: Korean. Gender: Male. Major: Pre-med. A pre-med Korean guy, who loves God. It's me. Born in Seoul, Korea in 1975. Came to California in 1991. Deep Springs '95. Seeks an attractive and Korean-speaking female companion. . . . Currently at the junction between nihilism and romanticism. Shall we blame Nietzche?

Joshua Kim   Fullerton, California

At Deep Springs, going home for a break is like eating a pancake for dinner. (Boy, I have to hate myself when I say things like that.) Deep Springs as an esoteric aphorism? One stops referring to DS as "Deep Springs College" after a while, and it almost becomes a cliché. Deep Springs as a cliché? Diversity, in all its glory and hyperbole, is a hot issue at Deep Springs, yet Nunn never spoke of diversity in his writings. The student body is also painfully uniform in its ethnicity, cultural background, and gender. Deep Springs as a self-contradiction? Who has ever questioned the need for such an institution as this? With a major portion of alumni going into law, medicine, politics, business, and education, DS seems to serve the society no differently than numerous other institutions of higher education. Deep Springs as a redundancy? One learns and teaches. One reads and writes. One works and plays. Deep Springs as a dichotomy? I am utterly enjoying myself in the construction of these overtly self-conscious, self reflecting passages. (Yeah, you should blame Nietzche.) Deep Springs as an ascetic self-indulgence? I learned to be sick and tired of myself. I also learned to make others be sick and tired of me. Deep Springs as an educational institution.

T. Abraham Lentner   Cedar Rapids, Iowa

I was raised on a plot of land surrounded by poplars. My sister Kim, one of my three siblings, and I
had to pick strawberries on summer afternoons. It was usually on a beautiful day and we'd both
rather play or do anything but work. We went out to the garden with our stainless steel bowls and
ate one out of each four we picked. We pretended we were world-famous soccer players enslaved
by jealously spiteful "bad-guys." Our hands dry with dirt-crust, and our faces smeared with juice,
we went into the house through the back porch and had dinner before the sun set.

T. Abraham Lentner   Cedar Rapids, Iowa

I drove from Iowa across the Great Plains and the Great Basin with my mother in the passenger seat of my gray-and-black pickup. I was excited and nervous, like I was when my mother used to drive me to middle school and I was looking forward to a new day. When we got to Las Vegas, I dropped her off at the airport and, too excited to stay there overnight, I headed for Deep Springs. Knowing that I will only be here for two years, the experience itself is like a journey, a transit from one point to another. Being separated from the time and schedules of the outside world, each day is its own; I can enjoy life here, the wonderful people here.

Fritz Donnelly   Redmond, Washington

In Michigan I learned how to play from a straight-haired girl who once gave me a birthday present, though it wasn't my birthday. Michigan was the first place I met children. In New Zealand and
Singapore, I had lived with adults, with pigs, and with spider limbed trees, but never had I lived with
people my age. I was so excited to see children, to talk with children, that every week in first grade
I told someone it was my birthday—a way of saying hello for a child just crawling out of his cara-
pace. Some weeks later my sister was born in Michigan, where we lived in a one-room apartment,
no bigger than an alleyway laundromat.

Fritz Donnelly   Redmond, Washington

I have been looking for toads. Spade-foot toads sleep beneath desert sands, coming to life when they hear the patter of rain on the desert roof. In the thin minutes that moisture remains pooled on the crust, the toads eat, croak, reproduce, lay eggs, and, as the pools disappear and tadpoles sprout from their eggs, the toads resubmerge to sleep for years until the next storm. I call out "Rumplestiltskin, Rumplestiltskin, Rumplestiltskin," in hopes of falling through the floor, to go down and see them.

Aron Fischer   Sausalito, California

I spent most of my childhood living at Green Gulch Farm, a Zen Buddhist community located near Muir Beach, California. Both of my parents are ordained as Buddhist priests; my father is presently one of the abbots, or head priests, of the San Francisco Zen Center, with which Green Gulch is affiliated, and my mother teaches fifth grade in nearby Mill Valley. I have a twin brother in art school and no other siblings. I came to Deep Springs because, having always attended school outside of Green Gulch, I wanted to participate as a full-fledged member in a community, because I figured that it is hard to go wrong living in the high desert, and because I didn't feel the need to fight my irrational desire to.

Aron Fischer   Sausalito, California

Sometime in my first few weeks at Deep Springs, a returning student said in a speech something like, "Deep Springs is, and it is many things; I don't feel like talking about it." I rolled my eyes at the time at what seemed like lazy pretension, but, living here, I have realized that he was articulating a legitimate reaction to the constant talking that goes on. Surrounded by desert, animals, and, most importantly, people by whom, like it or not, we can't help but be touched emotionally, we have the opportunity here to feel directly the effects of the things we do. My favorite things to do at Deep Springs are to hike, to write, and to labor in groups.

Mihir Kshirsagar   **Bombay, India**

I was born on the 10th of February 1977 in Bombay, India to Meenal and Eknath Kshirsagar. My childhood was spent in Bombay and Madras. In seventh grade I went to Rishi Valley, a boarding school founded by J. Krishnamurti, a philosopher in Andhra Pradesh, India. The nine years I spent in the Krishnamurti system of education, three in Madras and six in Rishi Valley, affected me very deeply. The system created an atmosphere of freedom and opportunity for me to grow and explore myself and the world around me.

Mihir Kshirsagar   Bombay, India

After high school I came directly to Deep Springs. I heard of Deep Springs through a guide to colleges just prior to the admissions deadline, and from the brief description I intuitively knew this place was the education of my dreams. Fortunately, the Applications Committee thought the same. My future after Deep Springs is undecided. I am interested in public policy and perhaps I shall pursue that. In the present I am enjoying my experience here and learning from it. I guess that is all that matters. While trekking through the 150 acres of alfalfa that my partner and I are responsible for irrigating, I don't think about my "experience" here, I simply experience it. When I get an opportunity to reflect on the "experience," on a break for instance, I sometimes don't believe it's true—it's such a total, intense experience that it feels unreal viewing it from the outside. I cannot imagine my life without Deep Springs.

Rosten Woo   Seattle, Washington

I tend to tie my identity up with place. When I first arrived here, I thought of myself as being from Seattle. From the city. Now that I've been here awhile, I've lost a lot of my connections back home, and I tend to think of myself as pretty rootless. Anyway, I've lived in the city my whole life. And that's the "city" city. Not the suburbs. So I guess I do still identify myself with places. My area code was 206 and I went to Garfield High School. I used to know more about record companies than publishing houses, but now it's the other way around. I'm probably gonna go to grad school when I finish undergrad. And I hope to live in China for a few years in-between. It's kind of scary to feel like you can plan ahead that far, like I'm already on the train. I'm not really all that interested in academia, but I've got this sinking suspicion that despite my efforts that's where I'll end up. Don't take that to mean I'm real comfortable about it. I'm not so much of a determinist as this makes me sound. Maybe I'll work in public service—a librarian, a social worker.

Rosten Woo   Seattle, Washington

The most important things I've learned here have all been political, like how to deal with people at slightly higher stakes than usual. This place can get kind of damaging, embittering. It's easy to get tied up in it, and when things screw up, you feel pretty responsible, which is a good thing overall. I have a lot of problems with a lot of the school's founding ideals, but one of the best things about the place is that it maintains this image of alterability. But there are a lot of different levels on which you can love it. A friend of mine was working barista at a café and one day this guy shows up wearing this Deep Springs T-shirt—Chris Thomas, who should have been in the class above me this year. She's kinda curious about it and when he comes up to order she says to him: "Hey, Deep Springs, a friend of mine's going there, did you go there, or did you graduate from there or . . . ?" He says to her, "I escaped."

Carson Thoreen   Seattle, Washington

I am about 5'10". I found it's a good height for many things: when cooking, the stove and counters come just above my waist, which is perfect; I have a good sense of balance that helps when climbing boulders; I'm allowed on both the adult and children's rides at the fair; most clothing fits me. I collect stuff that I call "gear" such as skis, climbing shoes, backpacks, notebooks, and bicycle parts, which are scattered around my room and hanging from my bed and walls. I've been 5'10" since 8th grade and don't plan to grow any more.

Carson Thoreen   Seattle, Washington

In the beginning months I wasn't sure why I came to Deep Springs, wanting to be a CompSci major and knowing the computers here are full of dust and react badly when you try to use them. My nose was constantly peeling from the desert sun and my hands were swollen from washing dishes in bleach water. Through the year I wrote papers on surrealism and dead poets, stories for a fiction class, took pictures, cooked regularly for sixty people, herded cattle, did some research on mathematical approximations of fault zones, installed an Ethernet 10T network, learned to drive stick, and built my bicycle. I now can't imagine having gone anywhere else.

John-Henry Behrens   West Hempstead, New York

I grew up on Long Island off the coast of New York. I left home at fourteen for Connecticut and boarding school. Four years later I arrived at Deep Springs, my home for the past two years. Last summer I was rummaging through my closet in my room back home and I came across a photo in a shoebox of photos from when I was a child. They all had that yellowy tinge that all old photos have, but this one in particular was different from all the rest. It was faded like the others, but I couldn't place the subject of the photograph, nor the period, for it seemed as though it was me standing there by that stream so very like the one that flowed past my grandparents' house in its prime, but if it was me I ought to have remembered being in the photograph, and if it was someone else, as it also seemed, then it was a strange thing indeed for someone over fifteen years ago to have been standing in a stream looking as if he were me. I was inclined to think that it was my father, but it didn't look anything like him. I left the photo in the shoebox with all of the other old photographs.

John-Henry Behrens   West Hempstead, New York

Spring nights when there was enough moonlight we'd climb up the ridge out back behind the college until we found a good spot to sit comfortably and look out over the valley. We'd all be silent,
watching each other's silhouettes until one of us felt something worth saying come out of his
mouth. Then someone else would pick up the line and make it a little longer and then another, on
and on, weaving we knew not what but damned pleased with the weaving. We got to know each
other's yarns like that, and we've all got our collections of knotty mementos up against the back wall
of some storage room inside our skulls, piled high, sitting around gathering dust. They're waiting for
when we're old and sitting in our rocking chairs trying to keep sleep from creeping up on us.

Zachary Herold   Oneonta, New York

My name is Zachary Lewis Herold, three names, one handed down from generations, a rupture from
the chain of Harold Herolds that preceded me; one the vestige of a once-removed clan, a forgotten
maiden name of a snapped branch in a genealogy; and, finally, a name selected from a baby names
dictionary, chosen for ring and the "z," admitting that this herald will be the last.

Zachary Herold   Oneonta, New York

Deep Springs has brought me many revisions, but now, on the edge of departure, I realize the shifts and turns fit the shape of a circle. When I arrived here, I listened to a Walkman; now, I hear birds. When I arrived here, I held that thoughts are not words, words are words, and the behest to speak is a plea for recognition. Now, I am open to silence.

Mark Rutschman-Byler   Chicago, Illinois

Mark Rutschman-Byler, SWM, 19 yr. old Argentine-born Quaker-raised queer writer, 5'10", blond curls, good nails, likes ancient Egypt, Bob Dylan, salads, nighttime walks, the Southwestern United States, chocolate w/hot coffee, wide open spaces, movement, silence, darkness, candles, ripped shoes, public transportation, unflickering flames, road trips, massage, marijuana in small doses when the energy is right, cassette tapes, used bookstores, unusually warm temperatures, order, fast pens, green, labor unions, silk, horses.

Mark Rutschman-Byler   Chicago, Illinois

Take watching the sunrise from inside my sleeping bag on top of a mountain it made no sense to climb with Jake, with Jamie, with not enough hot-dogs, with an "always-already" excess of beauty. Take Boomerang, at first a wet worm beneath me, shifting to a magnetic gallop. Take dust splattered lariats, the cries "Dally! Dally!" as the rope slaps soundly against calf-legs. Take touches in warm places, his beard scratching needles into my cheeks and my neck. Take eating tomatoes fresh from the garden, like apples, picked off the stalk as I walk into the din and the clatter of the chicken house, splattering feed into feeders while birds swoop around me and dust fills the air, fills the yellow dimension that sunset can bring.

Matthew Kwatinetz   Morganville, New Jersey

I was born in New Jersey and spent my whole life there before college. I went to a public high school that had a specialized program in performing arts, and I spent a good deal of my time involved in artistic activities. When I was first thinking about colleges, I never imagined that such a place as Deep Springs existed. I wanted to study philosophy and mathematics, as well as continue my artistic pursuits on the side. However, the opportunity to attend Deep Springs, and all that opportunity represented, demanded acceptance.

Matthew Kwatinetz   Morganville, New Jersey

One of the more potent experiences that I remember having while at Deep Springs was a horse-packing trip that John, Keith, Abe, Misha, and I took over the mountains into Death Valley. None of us were experienced horsepackers, and many of us were relatively new horsemen. After encouragement and planning sessions with Geoff Pope, the ranch manager, and Jack Newell, the college president, we set off through Soldier Pass together. I think that we were all fairly nervous; I know that I certainly was. We didn't make camp the first night until well after dark, and when we finally stumbled in, I'm sure that I wasn't the only one doubting our intelligence for having undertaken this trip without a more experienced hand along. A few days later, we rode back into the Valley, our spirits high after our adventures (and misadventures).

David Gregory   Paterson, New Jersey

I remember growing up in Illinois, in the small town where my mom was a teacher, my cousins
farmers; I remember blackberries around the old barn, pints of strawberries, and losing frisbees in
the corn fields—my mom was tall and she could find them for us. But most of my growing up was
in New Jersey, in that ever spreading desert of concrete and steel where it does not seem to be the
earth that sustains you. And now this California desert feels like home. Each place is a leg in the
journey of my whole; I'm struggling now to think them together. Bags of concrete make my shoul-
ders sag, as does all this brain freight. Though I'd rather carry both than either, when I can I take
the time to here and there set them down, and rise above.

David Gregory   Paterson, New Jersey

When I first came to Deep Springs three years ago, a student in the class above me spoke of how the mind could be blown away, like dandelion heads in the wind. These seeds fall on different soils. I love water and willows, as well as rock and desert brush; I love that I can walk my daily horizon. At Deep Springs my childhood notions of the earth and life have complicated, deepened; I want to build anew these systems which sustain us, these systems which we somehow lost touch with somewhere. I want to build houses with straw and mud and sticks to nourish myself and others, both from the earth and my hands. I want to create a life which sings, which dances on its whole foundation, which dances in cities and fields, on roads and rooftops. I embrace unlearning what we've been taught: that truth is found by breaking everything into its smallest pieces. Deep Springs has taught me how to break, and how hard it is to build.

Keith Hiestand   **Chesterton, Indiana**

I grew up in the small town of Chesterton, Indiana, a few miles from the southern shore of Lake
Michigan, an hour train-commute to downtown Chicago and equidistant to the heavy industry of
major steel-production plants and to the natural beauty of Indiana Dunes National Lakeshore.
Before Deep Springs, I studied for two years at a state magnet high school in Muncie, Indiana. The
bright sun and high-desert air of Deep Springs Valley have been a welcome contrast to the overcast
skies and frequent rain of Muncie.

Keith Hiestand   Chesterton, Indiana

A ranch and a farm and suburban lawn in the desert! At Deep Springs, water from the White Mountains feeds the alfalfa fields, our garden, and the crazy green lawns. The water runs from Wyman Canyon, from the convergence of Wyman and Crooked Creek into the headworks of the Deep Springs hydroelectric plant, into a closed canal and across the desert to the turbine and then to the lower reservoir. It reappears sometime later, carried in the wind by irrigation lines or dripping from a garden hose or spinning in circles above the main lawn. What is left runs on past the college, spinning out into the desert.

It is easy to allow the events and responsibilities of community life to draw you inside the main circle, inside buildings to wash pots, cook dinner, write a paper on a glowing computer screen. Still, some of my best times here have been while hiking or horseback riding or out for a walk under a clear night sky. The desert has a stillness and a beauty that can bring the greatest peace.

AFTERWORD

Some Thoughts on Neglected Water Taps

NO ONE CAN UNDERSTAND DEEP SPRINGS without reference to the "Grey Book" of the founder, Lucien Lucius Nunn. Deep Springs is a (usually) all-male junior college through which good, bad and mediocre students and faculty have passed. So what? Deep Springs is a cattle ranch. As a cattle ranch, Deep Springs is not especially efficient. How could it be? The wise, grizzled ranch manager often has one professional farmer to help him, but most of his other irrigators, ditch-diggers, feed men and roundup cattle-branders are novices who learn on the job—or not.

I myself have no idea as to whether on balance I was a good or bad feed man. I never overslept or broke anything. But I remember quite well the winter morning when the ranch manager, Mr. Holloway, whom I idolized, said to me with a grim little laugh, "Are you making a skating rink, Bill?" and I realized I'd forgotten to shut off water in one of the cattle troughs. I'm only grateful that no calf slipped on the ice and broke a leg.

I also remember the first time when as irrigator I noticed that one of the rainbirds wasn't spinning. If I didn't fix it, that patch of alfalfa would stay thirsty. So I shut down the wheel line, opened the rainbird in question, and discovered inside the incredibly compacted corpse of a mouse which had evidently gotten sucked into the intake valve, drowned, and crushed into a furry, cylindrical occlusion. What to do? Removing the plastic toothpick of my Swiss army knife, I pried the dead thing out. Then I pressured up the line again. Every rainbird whirled happily; every water-jet made a rainbow. I felt proud. I wiped the toothpick on my shirt and picked my teeth with it. Here was I, a pimply teenager unloved by girls, a clumsy, four-eyed sort with no previous experience of manual labor (my father and grandfather were both machine shop whizzes, and I'd never even been able to hammer a nail straight), and in spite of all this I'd actually been able to fix something. Probably Mr. Holloway could have done it in five seconds without even turning off the water; and he wouldn't have been impelled into any rituals of triumphant adolescent savagery. I must have wasted fifteen minutes on this operation. That's why I say that the ranch would undoubtedly turn a more consistent profit without students like me.

I remember the physical work I did in the valley with joy. It was all for a purpose, and we ourselves often got to decide how to perform it. We were responsible; we succeeded or failed, and the results directly affected our community. And everywhere around us, the land was lovely beyond description, a beauty that grew on me with the seasons. Sinking my left hand-hook into hay bales as I crouched on the bed of "my" 1953 Chevy feed truck, which I'd left in gear so that it bumbled across the desert by itself (a method of driving no doubt highly approved by the California Department of Motor Vehicles), I slashed twine, then kicked the alfalfa off into the snow. Black cows loomed beautifully in the fog, waiting to eat. In the spring everything would be olive-green; in the summer, grey and bright, with arrowheads twinkling at dusk. I remember petroglyphs and pictographs, snowy mountains and lizards in the heat; it was all heaven.

As for my academic experiences, well, I was the only student in Dr. Mawby's biology class. And when he'd say, "Does anyone know the phylum of the polychaete flatworm?" I'd look around to make sure, but "anyone" was always me. I was only a B student, but I loved Dr. Mawby for his immense knowledge, patience, and corny deadpan jokes. He was the perfect teacher. How could he not have been? I had every opportunity to learn, and no excuses. Sometimes we'd go to places in the valley or the mountains that Dr. Mawby knew (the land was his; he'd written the article on Death Valley for the *Britannica*); and he'd show me the living or fossilized truth of the words he'd just uttered in the classroom. Everything was whole and logical. That too was perfect.

At the request of another student from my home town, my philosophy teacher, Alan Paskow, hosted a series of sessions in "applied philosophy" in which we first defined the meaning of life, then built upon that definition to suggest specific improvements which we could make at Deep Springs itself. And we *were* Deep Springs; we were the minds and also the ditch-diggers. The place was ours. Within L.L. Nunn's gentle limits, we were free to make of it what we would.

I remember my solar energy teacher, Peter Lehmann. We spent the first semester studying thermodynamics. For the second semester we used thermodynamics to conceptualize a practical project which would be useful and also save the college energy. We decided to build a solar hot water system for the dairy barn. And we built it. Every now and then my nails went in straight. My friend Jake, who later became a mechanical engineer, deserves principal credit for the magnificent truss which still adorns the dairy barn roof. The solar collectors, alas, have long since become useless relics. Thus the typical doom of most Deep Springs projects, for each new student body reinvents the wheel. But they worked splendidly for a few years; it used to make me proud to see them.

About the female faculty I can only say that (as were many of my classmates) I was hopelessly in love with all of them. Peter's wife Carolyn Polese used to critique my short stories for me. Alan's wife Jackie was my French teacher, and I still remember the excitement of reading Gide, Malraux and Proust in the original—looking up every third word in the dictionary, to be sure, for I've never been good at languages. Sharon Schuman, who with her husband David taught English composition and public speaking, was fearsomely logical and hard to please. It was hard to get a sloppy composition past her. I was crazy about her.

I remember listening to David read his short stories aloud at night, and longing to write short stories just like him. (Jake wrote short stories, too, some of them quite beautiful and all of them sincere. At Deep Springs it was pretty ordinary to write prose in the morning and weld a truss in the afternoon.) I remember sitting down to dinner in the boarding house next to Dr. Mawby and his shy wife Diane, with some new question about why butterflies were related to shrimp; probably I was wearing the castoff coveralls I'd found in the "bonepile" downstairs, for I would have just come back from the feed run at that hour; the coveralls reeked of gasoline, dirt, blood and grease. Since I got up early for the morning run, I often slept in those coveralls. Come to think of it, I really must have smelled bad. But Dr. Mawby never said an unkind thing.

None of this would have any relevance without the Grey Book. The dream of L.L. Nunn was that his graduates would serve the world somehow. A good blacksmith served as well as a good President, Nunn said. What if that was true? What if my remembering or forgetting to turn off the water on the feed trough actually made a difference? (It obviously did.) What if philosophy could be applied right down to making suggestions about the curriculum? (It could.) What if Dr. Mawby really cared about helping me learn? (He liked me; he always helped me; he was my friend.) What if I could go out and do good? Of course I'd fail most of the time, just as I usually failed at Deep Springs. One student, a sullen gifted painter whom I admired mainly at a distance, because he detested me, even said that the point of Deep Springs was *learning how to fail*. And there's much truth in that. Often the rainbird will get stuck and we can't figure out how to remove the dead mouse. But we can also learn *from* our failures, and try in our small way to do good.

A few years ago in south Thailand I met a twelve-year-old girl whose father had sold her into prostitution in order to pay for a new roof. I asked this child if she liked her job, and she told me she didn't, because the men often hit her, and sometimes she got diseases. So I kidnapped her and put her in a girls' school in Bangkok. It was scary, and I might have failed; I might have left the water tap on and gotten her and me hurt. But I didn't. I helped that girl. I didn't solve all her problems, but I got her to a place where she could choose what to do next. And we tested her; she didn't have AIDS. One of my guiding principles in that kidnapping was the maxim we'd derived in the applied philosophy class at Deep Springs: We ought to identify and empathize with the physical and moral order of the universe, whatever that may be, and we should help others do the same. It was that second clause which operated here. I just did my best to take her someplace where the universe might be easier for her to empathize with. Sometimes doing my best has brought about disasters, but (as Alan Paskow convinced me in his Heidegger-Wittgenstein class) it's almost always better to do your best, and do *something,* than to do nothing out of fear of making mistakes or causing evil. I'm not talking about mindless, self-righteous activism. I'm talking about doing the best job you can to fix a problem you really *know* about. The blacksmith shouldn't walk right into the Oval Office and be President. He's got to do a little reading and flesh-pressing first. For that matter, the President is unlikely to make a horseshoe on his first attempt. People who want to ban female circumcision without ever having seen it, or people who just know that the Serbs are bad because the television says so, may well be correct about both issues. But if in the background some water trough unmentioned by the television has begun to overflow, those do-gooders might not see it; and their neglect might cause harm. Deep Springs taught me to go and see things for myself, to get the best information about problems I could, to worry a lot and plan a lot, until the unfamiliar became comprehensible, and only then (crossing my fingers and hoping for the best) to *do* my best. For what does a Deep Springs education ask of us, if not to do our best? Since we've been given every opportunity, we now have no excuses.

WILLIAM T. VOLLMANN
Sacramento, California
February 2000

The photographs for
The Students of Deep Springs College
were made in October 1995 and April 1996.
All are gelatin silver-chloride contact prints
made from 8 x 10-inch negatives
except for the frontispiece,
which was made from an 8 x 20-inch negative.

Designed by PM Design Studios
Typeset in Monotype Centaur and Monotype Bembo
and printed in quadtone on 200 gsm Job Parilux
from laser-scanned 600-line screen negatives
by Salto
Bound by Roswell Bookbinding

For information regarding other titles by Lodima Press:
P.O. Box 367 Revere, Pennsylvania 18953 USA
Telephone: 610-847-2007   Fax: 610-847-2373
www.lodimapress.com